A HAIKU DIARY

年

by Rita Randazzo

Sprezzatura Books
South Burlington, Vermont

Sprezzatura Books
New Renaissance Press
8 Woodside Drive
South Burlington, VT 05403

ISBN: 9780970827944
Library of Congress Control Number: 2010918074

Drawings on front and back covers, the Seasons
pages, and author's photograph by Joe Randazzo

Front cover character – Year (and Age)
Back cover character - Life

"It adds to the pleasure of life to notice things."

Barbara Pym

Other books by Rita Randazzo:

Fifty/50
His/Hers: Mars & Venus Write Poetry
    (with Joe Randazzo)
A Passion for Flavor (with Eve Plociennik)
Feeding Herself
The Country Kitchen Cookbook

For Joe, my husband, who looked at a handwritten haiku journal I gave him for our Silver Anniversary and saw this book in it. From the Japanese characters he drew, to the design of the pages, to the mechanics of laying out the manuscript, his talent and loving care are everywhere evident. *Joseph* means *he shall add.* Joe Randazzo adds to the joy in this world.

When I got a calendar in book form as a Christmas gift, I wondered what to do with it. A very attractive volume, it had lovely color plates of country gardens and antique baskets, and small lined squares for each day of the year. I decided to use it as a diary and note a daily highlight to remind me to pay attention to the flow of life.

The squares were not big enough for the conventional ramblings of a typical journal, so I chose to write little poems instead. I've been writing haiku poetry since I was a teenager, and the form comes naturally to me. Spareness has always appealed to me; in constriction there is a counterintuitive freedom. I began on December 30, my sister's birthday, and when the year came to an end I wasn't ready to stop. The diary ran through January 10th of the next year, and I ran with it.

In the years since I completed my diary, I have learned a lot more about haiku, and I can clearly see that many of my little poems are not true haiku at all. I agree with Jack Kerouac, who taught that haiku lines are about the breath, not the syllables. The rigid three-line, 5-7-5 syllable count is not in the spirit of the great Japanese haiku masters like Issa and Basho. Each line should be one breath, not a fixed number of syllables.

Even so, I still like my Haiku Diary. There is something satisfying in the persistence with which I kept it up, the faithfulness of the practice, and the memories each tiny writing holds. It is doubly satisfying to reproduce it here, to share with others who might, like me, see beauty in the small and simple and imperfect.

Rita Randazzo
December 1, 2010

冬

WINTER

一月

Monday, December 30

Stripped and bare of
finery this gray Monday:
The poor Christmas tree.

Tuesday, December 31

Oh, Man loves wine and
wine loves Man, but which love might
be the hungrier?

Wednesday, January 1—New Year's Day

New day dawns, new year
yawns and stretches sleepily.
Start anew now: How?

Thursday, January 2

Snapping logs ablaze,
woodstove warming chilly paws,
How Miss Puss loves it!

Friday, January 3

Hemlock trees arow
keep each other company
through lonely winter.

Saturday, January 4

The rain falls - false spring -
Nature is unkind to lie
so to the squirrel.

Sunday, January 5

How I am grown fat
with sloth and gluttony: It's
past time for virtue!

Monday, January 6

My beloved's day
of birth means precious hours to
Show him how I care.

Tuesday, January 7

An ancient lady
wants "to go" but wakes up each
morning just the same.

Wednesday, January 8

Molten yellow light
gilds bare branches that were gray
just yesterday - Sun!

Thursday, January 9

Oh, confident crow,
big strutting blackbird, you think
you own my front yard!

Friday, January 10

The ground is still bare:
If I could choose the weather
it would snow and snow!

Saturday, January 11

Wood warms us two times,
once in the cutting and once
in the burning: True!
~Henry David Thoreau~

Sunday, January 12

We can celebrate
the way nature has made us:
oh joy of the flesh.

Monday, January 13

It did snow, a bit.
It will snow again, I hope;
but never enough.

Tuesday, January 14

Today no squirrels
come to eat sunflower seeds:
Rain, rain, yet more rain.

Wednesday, January 15

Ice flowers, fingers
of frost write January
on cold window panes.

Thursday, January 16

A coat of satin,
motorboat purr, jungle eyes:
Yes, such is the cat.

Friday, January 17

The place you want to
be when you need to be there:
A hospital bed.

Saturday, January 18

Frost pictures and sand
castles - transient beauty
is here and then gone.

Sunday, January 19

Take me to a new
world, give me another life:
Let me read a book.

Monday, January 20—MLK Jr. Day

Great men have a day
named for them: We plain folk
have only our lives.

Tuesday, January 21

Our houseplants and we
struggle along together
to survive winter.

Wednesday, January 22

Savory odors
fill our little house: making
chicken soup today.

Thursday, January 23

Confusion: As if
it were night and day at once,
or noon at midnight.

Friday, January 24

When I stroke my cat,
her fur is hand-happy, my
hand is fur-happy.

Saturday, January 25

Seeds for the tiny
chickadees: oh, no - greedy
squirrels steal them all.

Sunday, January 26

Gentlemen callers
for Puss, but in vain: only
humans' love for her.

Monday, January 27

Bright blood flows from me,
my never to be born babes,
month after month - gone.

Tuesday, January 28

Fairy frosting on
the trees, sugar diamonds,
crystal stars of snow.

Wednesday, January 29

If lying is wrong
and caring is right, what then
is a caring lie?

Thursday, January 30

Wash dishes, clean the
litter box: obligation
and privilege, too.

Friday, January 31

Don't want to turn the
calendar page for love of
January's cat.

二
月

Saturday, February 1

Snow shaker sky:　through
the window I see a world
newly white and mute.

Sunday, February 2

Doves flutter at the
glass door, reminding us that
we are their keepers.

Monday, February 3

Twenty-four years now:
Marriage is the adventure
of my life's journey.

Tuesday, February 4

One squirrel scampers
to and fro, burying Cheese
Doodles in the snow.

Wednesday, February 5

Some buds are never
meant to bloom, but only to
wither and to die.

Thursday, February 6

Animal tracks in
the snow end abruptly: Where
did the creature go?

Friday, February 7

The week winds down like
a clock: Saturday, Sunday,
our chance just to STOP.

Saturday, February 8

Saturday alone:
A light snow is falling and
the phone doesn't ring.

Sunday, February 9

At l'heure bleu the snow
is indeed - blue - as summer
sky, summer water.

Monday, February 10

Snow is blue at dusk,
magic colors of twilight
before light is gone.

Tuesday, February 11

My cat will play games,
rugby and baseball as well
as old cat and mouse.

Wednesday, February 12

My mother is like
a warming woodstove: Draw close
and be comforted.

Thursday, February 13

Why did I not see
when three years ago a moose
walked down our street?

Friday, February 14—Valentine's Day

My heart is mine to
keep or give; I give it so
joyfully to you.

Saturday, February 15

Yes, Scott Peck, life is
difficult; there is surely
no peace, only rest.

Sunday, February 16

Snow dunes shape the world
of our back yard, white sugar
beach in Wonderland.

Monday, February 17

I'm in love with the
Boboli bread man for his
cute Italian nose.

Tuesday, February 18

One sere leaf endures
on the apple tree, winter
brown but still around.

Wednesday, February 19

Horace Silver plays.
Music and the open road;
let's just keep driving.

Thursday, February 20

Paws like boxing gloves;
my mitten-toed kitty
has VERY big feet!

Friday, February 21

A walk in the snow,
all alone with the pleasure
of my pink earmuffs.

Saturday, February 22

White Zinfandel is
the color of pink topaz:
jewel of a wine.

Sunday, February 23

The cat is restless,
goes from window to window.
Does she look for spring?

Monday, February 24

Need to go, don't want
to go; too late now since we
bought the plane tickets.

Tuesday, February 25

Mother let go her
party balloons; they took her
along to the clouds.

Wednesday, February 26

~ For Ed~
Your death does not touch
me half so deeply as did
your life: Goodbye, friend.

Thursday, February 27

"Weary, stale, flat, and
unprofitable": Shakespeare
knew about the blues.

Friday, February 28

A cup of tea, some
conversation; good neighbors,
I'm glad you're next door.

Saturday, February 29

Leap Day: If I were
born forty years ago, I'd
be just ten today!

三月

Sunday, March 1

Minestrone soup
and rough bread: good honest lunch
on a snowy day.

Monday, March 2

Winter tragedy:
We're all out of wood and the
furnace doesn't work.
(p.s. The wood man's in Florida.)

Tuesday, March 3

It's Fat Tuesday and
I'm on a diet since I
am already fat!

Wednesday, March 4

Lent: Contrary Joe
plans to give up abstinence
for the forty days.

Thursday, March 5

Two crosspatches can
get into a fight about
nothing in no time.

Friday, March 6

We can all smell Spring
coming: cats, birds, squirrels, trees,
and housebound humans.

Saturday, March 7

In Vermont, we have
to slog thorough oceans of mud
to get to our Spring.

Sunday, March 8

e.e. cummings would
not have thought spring in Vermont
mud-luscious, would he?

Monday, March 9

The dentist is done
at last; I can close my mouth
and go numbly home.

Tuesday, March 10

A day of pain, but
not pain only; TV, a
book, and red wine, too.

Wednesday, March 11

How can I leave my
cat? I have no way to tell
her I'm coming back.

Thursday, March 12

Where is my bookworm
pin, my Methodist medal?
In Lost Things Heaven.

Friday, March 13

Surprise snowfall; I
lay awake watching snowplow
lights flash through the night.

Saturday, March 14

Red onion, carrot
ribbons, tang of vinegar:
Salad is so good!

Sunday, March 15

Big diet failure:
I haven't lost weight and I
crave a BAD pizza.

Monday, March 16

Last poem from home -
we leave in early morning -
Goodbye, normal life!

Tuesday, March 17

Midair jitterbug
in a prop plane: Wish I were
watching Donahue.

Wednesday, March 18

Our first day as guests:
Will we stink after two more
or remain fragrant?

Thursday, March 19

Welcome to SC,
where Henry Wedemeyer
reigns o'er his domain.

Friday, March 20

Shopping with Mother,
hitting the sales, laughing at
our pleasure in it.

Saturday, March 21

Mr. Sundance horse
kindly permitted me to
ride him for a while.

Sunday, March 22

Poor woman asleep
in phone booth, screened by a
handkerchief curtain.

Monday, March 23

Yesterday a plane
crashed: Today I will fly
home still, never fear.

Tuesday, March 24

Home again, picking
up the dropped stitches in
the same old knitting.

Wednesday, March 25

A lost day, spent in
trying to regain balance
and sobriety.

Thursday, March 26

Pleasure to me is
a new mug for tea, in black
with white polka dots.

Friday, March 27

Empty rooms, and I
haven't strength enough to fill
the space with my self.

Saturday, March 28

Here it comes again!
A spring snow, catapulting
us back to winter.

Sunday, March 29

Snowlight shines through the
bedroom window, paling the
darkness of our night.

Monday, March 30

She who has been too
lazy to shop must eat weird
things that come in cans.

Tuesday, March 31

The month of March has
lasted forever; I am
ready for April.

SPRING

四
月

Wednesday, April 1

I see that I must
battle for the right to be
my own sort of fool.

Thursday, April 2

Already fat, two
robins plunder muddy soil
for winter-thin worms.

Friday, April 3

April showers here
may appear as snow. Thank God
I live in Vermont!

Saturday, April 4

Home Shopping Club: I
watch the world's goods parade by
and reject them all.

Sunday, April 5

Peril again, sunk
in the fear of a husband's
stark mortality.

Monday, April 6

In the morning, geese
winging their V-shaped way
to open water.

Tuesday, April 7

Peeling potatoes
is easier than fixing
my banking mistake!

Wednesday, April 8

First experience
of talking with "my" lawyer:
I will die someday.

Thursday, April 9

Gray cloud of fear and
guilt settles around my sad
shoulders like a cloak.

Friday, April 10

Be careful when you
wish for a break in routine:
You may not like it.

Saturday, April 11

World full of strange things:
Joe in the hospital and
snow in mid-April.

Sunday, April 12

Oh wine is such a
comfort, it almost holds your
hand: Respect it well.

Monday, April 13

My sister's anguish
is a cold stone in my throat:
I can't swallow it.

Tuesday, April 14

I was tightly in
control until I touched
his hair in goodbye.

Wednesday, April 15

How frightening that
my husband can hurt himself
with his very thoughts.

Thursday, April 16

Wake up, my human!
If you have a cat you don't
need an alarm clock.

Friday, April 17—Good Friday

Yet another snow;
the hemlocks bow their heads like
cowled penitents.

Saturday, April 18—Passover

Our kitty likes to
sprawl upon the stock pages:
must be a Fat Cat.

Sunday, April 19—Easter

Easter means nothing
to me; I don't feel part of
this Resurrection.

Monday, April 20

What good is "normal"
life, so fervently wished
for and yet so stale?

Tuesday, April 21

Only when it broke
did I throw away a lamp
I've had thirty years.

Wednesday, April 22

I have only to
tense my standing-up muscles
and Puss jumps off me.

Thursday, April 23

Mr. and Mrs.
Mallard have made our skating
rink their paddling pond.

Friday, April 24

Slender spears, first green
of spring, chives are the last left
alive in autumn.

Saturday, April 25

April showers are
fine, but not when they end up
on the cellar floor!

Sunday, April 26

Brand new bird feeders:
will they foil acrobatic
and greedy squirrels?

Monday, April 27

Florid, flow red, the
raucous strawberry screams of
hot summer ahead.

Tuesday, April 28

Cooking meat today,
it seemed so ugly that
I don't want dinner.

Wednesday, April 29

Many cars next door:
I think someone is being
born as I write this.

Thursday, April 30

The dream of jumping
off a building comes true when
I am wide awake.

五
月

Friday, May 1

My whole family
is in trouble: I am in
the hurricane's eye.

Saturday, May 2

Blackbird Mafia:
Grackles are the hoodlums of
avian culture.

Sunday, May 3

The men drive Ms. Finch
from the feeder: She finds a
higher, harsher perch.

Monday, May 4

First picnic of spring;
windy cold, hot almond tea
and turkey on rolls.

Tuesday, May 5

Both my mothers are
wounded; one is close, one far.
I do what I can.

Wednesday, May 6

Laundry and dishes,
cooking what husband wishes;
busy housewife me.

Thursday, May 7

Mom is seventy -
how can it be - when I am
still her needful child?

Friday, May 8

I must believe that
tomorrow's me can be, yes,
better than today's.

Saturday, May 9

Young grass, new leaves on
every tree; so very
many shades of green.

Sunday, May 10—Mother's Day

Holding a newborn
baby in my arms; pleasure
keen as a knife thrust.

Monday, May 11

His moods wash over
him like ocean waves, go in
and out like the tide.

Tuesday, May 12

Dandelion lawn:
Why ever are these golden
flowers called weeds?

Wednesday, May 13

July day in May;
hot breeze worries the apple
tree, barely in bud.

Thursday, May 14

Surveyor's red flag
says that our woods will soon fall
victim to progress.

Friday, May 15

Claudia and the
Cardinal dine together
at Café Birdseed.

Saturday, May 16

If I fully live,
when life is done with me I
will be done with it.

Sunday, May 17

Clambering over
purple rocks by blue water
on a spring morning...

Monday, May 18

The sun is playing
hide and seek today, peeping
in and out the clouds.

Tuesday, May 19

The world's two greatest
meals: Moo Shu Chicken and Mom's
macaroni cheese.

Wednesday, May 20

Lilacs begin their
brief and fragrant life; the bees
and I salute them.

Thursday, May 21

Whence comes self esteem?
To feel good must one do good?
Or look good? Who knows?

Friday, May 22

Robin takes a bath,
feathers aruffle on his
fat, rusty-red breast.

Saturday, May 23

Holiday weekend -
all possibility now,
over much too soon.

Sunday, May 24

It was 91
yesterday; this morning we
made a fire. Too weird!

Monday, May 25—Memorial Day

Alas, I do grow
older and fatter each day,
and I do despair.

Tuesday, May 26

Bad news, the worst news:
In-laws coming soon for a
visit. I will hide.

Wednesday, May 27

I hold up a hand
mirror to watch hummingbirds
and not startle them.

Thursday, May 28

Poor fly! He buzzed
into my house and met his
fate: The cat ate him.

Friday, May 29

Life without wine can
be fine. (Give up a little
and I gain a lot.)

Saturday, May 30

We can smell neighbors'
dinners cooking on the grill
as they must smell ours.

Sunday, May 31

May slides into June,
the year unfolding to its
own ruthless design.

六月

Monday, June 1

A lone Cyclamen
flower has braved this cold
day to show her face.

Tuesday, June 2

She who has been too
lazy to shop, and has no
cans, orders take-out.

Wednesday, June 3

Earrings, necklaces;
gold, gems, and silver pretties:
the Greedy Guts strike!

Thursday, June 4

Wasps and hornets and
bees, we are sorry to slay
you in self defense.

Friday, June 5

I can feel in my
fingers, feet, knees that the air
is preparing rain.

Saturday, June 6

The hemlock trees are
growing, their boughs outlined
in pale green newness.

Sunday, June 7

What do you call the
bestest mother in the world?
Answer: Optimum!

Monday, June 8

We say Goodbye, and
I learn a farewell can be
exhilarating.

Tuesday, June 9

Beatific day,
so glorious it hurts to
know the sun will set.

Wednesday, June 10

Blowzy peonies,
the pink of cotton candy;
outrageous flowers.

Thursday, June 11

We break in the new
lounge chairs, drink wine on the deck,
get mosquito bites.

Friday, June 12

Barking dogs ... children's
happy racket ... lawn mowers:
Suburban Summer.

Saturday, June 13

In the market, half
the women I saw wore blue;
bright turquoise bazaar.

Sunday, June 14

The heat is a weight,
a prison, pressing around
me, shutting the door.

Monday, June 15

This too, too solid
flesh is too fleshy and not
solid at all. Damn!

Tuesday, June 16

Abundant basil
suggests summer meals with oil,
pasta, tomatoes.

Wednesday, June 17

We've trained Puss
to misbehave for the praise
we give when she stops.

Thursday, June 18

Butterfly day: their
yellow, orange, and purple
flower our woods walk.

Friday, June 19

Kitty falls asleep
with her catnip toy on her
head like an ice bag.

Saturday, June 20

Many muggy days,
and then: welcome, delicious
cool air comes again.

Sunday, June 21—Father's Day

My Dad – difficult,
disappointing (like me) – but
he's mine and I'm his.

Monday, June 22

I measured my
height to see if I am old
enough yet to shrink.

Tuesday, June 23

They say it's better
to travel hopefully than
it is to arrive.

Wednesday, June 24

Wu-wei, non-action
of Tao: Be still, let life
happen to itself.

Thursday, June 25

My eyes would only
look inward today, and I
therefore saw nothing.

Friday, June 26

What I need right now
is a golden cross on a
chain to comfort me.

Saturday, June 27

Only three weeks 'til
the much-dreaded visit; it
will come all too soon.

Sunday, June 28

Waking in the night,
again and again, to find
my cat there with me.

Monday, June 29

There is nothing good
about pain; like the wasp, it
is known by its sting.

Tuesday, June 30

Dropped by a bird,
the seed has taken root and...
future sunflower?

夏

SUMMER

七月

Wednesday, July 1—Canada Day

Canada, phooey:
We always get lost and are
insulted in French.

Thursday, July 2

"Love is not a hot
potato that you can throw
out of the window."
~old Russian proverb~

Friday, July 3

Spotted horse, chipmunk
and rabbit – We met them all
in their woods today.

Saturday, July 4

Independence Day:
Would that all creatures were free
of cruel masters.

Sunday, July 5

Basket of pine cones,
treasure from the forest on
our kitchen table.

Monday, July 6

July is being
kind so far; dulcet days and
windows-open nights.

Tuesday, July 7

Fickle cardinals!
They have deserted us for
our neighbors' feeder.

Wednesday, July 8

Relentless pursuit
with sharp instruments by a
fiend in blue mascara.

Thursday, July 9

Lying on the floor,
"It is irrational to
move," the Frenchman said.

Friday, July 10

Golden haired, brown
eyed girlflower: Susan
grows in our garden.

Saturday, July 11

Nothing makes females
happier than losing five
pounds, I'm sad to say.

Sunday, July 12

Modern families
sing Happy Birthday to an
answering machine.

Monday, July 13

When there's no other
place, I can hide behind my
face, falsely smiling.

Tuesday, July 14

Finches fly away
in panic, not knowing the
cat is behind glass.

Wednesday, July 15

Worn down, tired out,
done in; I need a mommy
to take care of me.

Thursday, July 16

Be still inside! Sit
quietly and look around,
as one with the breeze.

Friday, July 17

Baby hands, tiny
dimpled knuckles dented like
bread dough, soft as soft.

Saturday, July 18

We are invaded,
and welcome the enemy,
hoping to find friends.

Sunday, July 19

Oh, the pain, having
strange women in my kitchen
just being helpful.

Monday, July 20

They depart, leaving
me so empty and filled
my tears are like wine.

Tuesday, July 21

Puddy hates me now,
scratching my face in pique at
strangers in her house.

Wednesday, July 22

Swinburne's Sunflower
has just showed her face, not
yet weary of time.

Thursday, July 23

Two robins vanquish
a jay; two women with strong
teeth bite me in half.

Friday, July 24

What has changed since
I last saw my friend to make
our hug so heartfelt?

Saturday, July 25

Three little boys crowd
'round the tall man; he kneels to
match their size. He sighs.

Sunday, July 26

A monumental
erection! Sexy new ham
antenna out back.

Monday, July 27

Silver wand waving
in a light breeze; will real wind
doom the antenna?

Tuesday, July 28

When Miss Puss withdraws
she's incommunicato:
It's catastrophic!
(and cataclysmic!)

Wednesday, July 29

Care well for a plant,
it will blossom for you; a
person, maybe not.

Thursday, July 30

Sick, sick, very sick.
To and fro to the bathroom.
Very, very, sick.

Friday, July 31

Rainy 5 p.m.,
waiting for Joe to bring home
the bacon (no, wine).

八
月

Saturday, August 1

Joe eats fruit all day
like a monkey, but he wants
to lose puppy fat.

Sunday, August 2

Doe and two fawns — long
frozen moment — gone with a
flash of three white flags.

Monday, August 3

A blow to the heart:
Lovely ethnic clothes are not
so lovely on me!

Tuesday, August 4

A tornado watch
does not always end in grief,
nor do strange phone calls.

Wednesday, August 5

Computer magic:
Enter three hard-done pages
and watch them vanish.

Thursday, August 6

Windows down in the
morning; seal up night's chill for
the hot day ahead.

Friday, August 7

A juicy novel,
a glass of white wine, and moi:
Paradise enow.

Saturday, August 8

Golden finch picking
sunflower seeds from inside
the golden blossom.

Sunday, August 9

Restless husband prowls
the house like a great cat; I
send him to the woods.

Monday, August 10

My mother didn't
want to talk with me Sunday:
I know it, somehow.

Tuesday, August 11

To be one of the
good guys you must rescue the
spider, not kill her.

Wednesday, August 12

Ragged sunflower –
ravaged by birds, squirrels –
hangs its dying head.

Thursday, August 13

Beheaded now, the
sunflower drops one last seed:
It will rise again.

Friday, August 14

Watching Home Shopping
at 4 a.m. – Who are these
sleepless ring-buyers?

Saturday, August 15

Green glass vase holds tall
yellow glads, the flower of
jolly funerals.

Sunday, August 16

The gladiolas –
dying flowers chase new buds
up and up the stem.

Monday, August 17

Afloat in a bowl,
orange and improbable,
the tiger lily.

Tuesday, August 18

Little wanderer,
turning life inside out and
making Top Cat mad.

Wednesday, August 19

To save the kitten's
life we must risk it: Painful
godspeed at the pound.

Thursday, August 20

Pale-faced friend boards
her first plane, facing terror,
sixty-eight years old.

Friday, August 21

The phabulous phlox,
in candy pink bloom, looking
simply phantastic!

Saturday, August 22

We shall have only
as many apples as the
squirrels choose to leave.

Sunday, August 23

The dream is made flesh
in a tangle of limbs and
possibilities.

Monday, August 24

Tomatoes, red and
green, festoon the vines as they
ripen day by day.

Tuesday, August 25

Misery of heat;
air to choke on, not to breathe;
snake in the cellar.

Wednesday, August 26

I want the last two
cookies, but save them for Joe:
Good deed of the day!

Thursday, August 27

Outdoor table with
candles; three "old folks" enjoy
dinner al fresco.

Friday, August 28

Some tame gazelle ... some
gentle dove; Something to love,
oh, something to love!
~Thomas Haynes Bayly~

Saturday, August 29

At last the heat has
broken; at last the windows
are wide, wide open.

Sunday, August 30

Covered bridge in the
morning, argument at night:
day in a married life.

Monday, August 31

Red sugar-water
lures the shy green hummingbird
close to us giants.

九月

Tuesday, September 1

Bad year for apples:
Those spared by the squirrels have
fallen to the worms.

Wednesday, September 2

Empty nest again;
useless leaves, twigs fall away.
No baby this month.

Thursday, September 3

Rain has watered our
plants and filled the birdbath, but
I did the dishes.

Friday, September 4

Pain overwhelms me;
I am no more than vessel
for the agony.

Saturday, September 5

First hot dinner since
Wednesday; I try to eat
Slowly ... to savor.

Sunday, September 6

Abandoned for a
gun show, I feel petulant!
I will make him pay!

Monday, September 7

Fine picnic in the
park: one special hour can wipe
out a whole bad week.

Tuesday, September 8

Graceful and serene,
Miss Puss stretches in the sun,
abandoned to bliss.

Wednesday, September 9

Red sliced tomato,
just plucked from the vine, startles
us with its fragrance.

Thursday, September 10

Dark at 4 p.m.,
thunderstorm lashes windows
with furious rain.

Friday, September 11

Three wildflowers in
a tiny red glass bottle:
very Shibui.

Saturday, September 12

Erotic daydreams —
torment and pleasure —
unreel in my brain.

Sunday, September 13

Strange people come to
paw through my neighbor's discards:
a Sunday yard sale.

Monday, September 14

Soap operas are
the last refuge of lazy,
romantic women.

Tuesday, September 15

Each day the same folks
visit my house: Talk shows are
easy company.

Wednesday, September 16

Sleepwalking through my
life from meal to meal, drink to
drink, and book to book.

Thursday, September 17

Keep doing what you've
doing and you'll keep getting
what you've been getting.

Friday, September 18

Hear my husband laugh
at TV cartoons, grownup
tickled by child's play.

Saturday, September 19

The chenille plant is
coifed in red dreadlocks, mass of
mad reggae flowers.

Sunday, September 20

Chinese couple jogs
down the street, waving gaily
to all the neighbors.

Monday, September 21

I help Joe pick out
new clothes: sweaters, flannel shirts,
and very wild ties.

Tuesday, September 22

Baking apple pie
on the first day of autumn,
making memories.

Wednesday, September 23

What Eden is this?
Great Blue Heron on a roof,
crayon-colored hills.

Thursday, September 24

Making cordial with
brandy and wild blackberries
we picked yesterday.

Friday, September 25

Left behind by The
Woodsman, I am glad enough
just to vegetate.

Saturday, September 26

Could I defend well
my life as I have lived it?
There's no time to lose.

Sunday, September 27

Together we turn
a basket of wormy fruit
to fine apple crisp.

Monday, September 28

Golden glass of
rose and garnet wines dazzle
eyes first, tongue second.

Tuesday, September 29

As gorgeous as the
lipstick-red maples, patches
of dark evergreen.

Wednesday, September 30

Man drinks the first glass,
first glass drinks the second, and
third glass drinks the man.
~Old Spanish proverb~

秋

AUTUMN

十月

Thursday, October 1

Close thine eyes to his
countenance; close thine ears to
his words. Watch his hands.
~Old Turkish proverb~

Friday, October 2

Marriage is like the
fire in a woodstove: Tend it
or it dies on you.
~New Vermont proverb~

Saturday, October 3

A jewel wrapped in
plain brown paper – a bright green
geode – Kiwifruit.

Sunday, October 4

Two weeks to do as
we please has spoiled us: We want
it all, forever.

Monday, October 5

gold finches, golden
leaves – which do I see? – tumbling
from the maple tree

Tuesday, October 6

Clouds like meringue float
in a blue sky pie above
colored-sprinkle hills.

Wednesday, October 7

I'll go for it as
soon as I build up a good
head of self-esteem.
                    (Courtesy RW & JR)

Thursday, October 8

seventy degrees ...
soft air ... bright sun on red leaves ...
Indian Summer

Friday, October 9

Lovely autumn rain,
gray day pleasure in tune with
my melancholy

Saturday, October 10

Overnight, our own
maples have donned party clothes
of yellow and red.

Sunday, October 11

Leaves brighten apace,
fall to the ground, are raked up:
And then it's winter.

Monday, October 12—Columbus Day

Hucks playing hooky,
exploring like Columbus,
we claim the day off.

Tuesday, October 13

Orange pumpkins, red
and yellow leaves: What colors
God has made for us!

Wednesday, October 14

Lord Jesus Christ, Son
of God, have mercy on me,
a sinner. Amen.

Thursday, October 15

"A person must not
realize himself at the
expense of others."
~Christopher Bryant~

Friday, October 16

Drifts of painted leaves
on the lawn wait quietly
like new-fallen snow.

Saturday, October 17

Baking cookies for
our neighbor who's lost her mom,
just to say sorry.

Sunday, October 18

Oh, how I hate an
emotional phone call from
my mother-in-law!

Monday, October 19

It is dark now when
we wake and pry ourselves out
of the warm, warm bed.

Tuesday, October 20

Grim faces at the
dentist's office: I have been
a very bad girl.

Wednesday, October 21

I seem to believe
youth is a country I can
find my way back to.

Thursday, October 22

Hunting proves nothing
except that men can pull a
trigger and deer can't.

Friday, October 23

Pro Life or Pro Choice
is not a question – Are not
all women for life?

Saturday, October 24

I have that "Today
is the first day of the rest
of my life" feeling.

Sunday, October 25

Life is an onion,
they say; you peel it and weep.
My eyes are stinging.

Monday, October 26

Politics is the
pursuit of power in the
absence of virtue.

Tuesday, October 27

Generation gap:
'cause the young want more room and
the old want more time.
~Rock Brynner~

~The 3-poem Anniversary Cycle~

Wednesday, October 28

I was seventeen
when I chose you for my own.
I choose you today.

Thursday, October 29

These twenty-nine years:
so good, so bad, so much our
particular us.

Friday, October 30

How can I tell all
I feel for you? I must let
my life itself speak.

Saturday, October 31—Halloween

Ghosties and goblins,
beasties and bats, graveyard ghouls
and demon black cats.

十
一
月

Sunday, November 1

"You (poets) don't have
to be right, all you have to
do is be candid."
~Allen Ginsberg~

Monday, November 2

Reading the Beats, 1
go back, back to sad sixteen
and Jack Kerouac.

Tuesday, November 3

In the voting booth
middle-aged eyes had trouble
seeing the future.

Wednesday, November 4

An angry husband
trying so hard not to let
the storm consume him.

Thursday, November 5

I would love to know
of my past lives, so clearly
the soul's history.

Friday, November 6

Middle-aged women
made over on TV look
reborn and relieved.

Saturday, November 7

Cold night for the cat
who wakes me up to let her
under my blanket.

Sunday, November 8

Joe rakes leaves as the
snow sifts down: The seasons are
overlapping now.

Monday, November 9

November doldrums –
gray skies spiked with sometime sun –
when joy's elusive.

Tuesday, November 10

Piling on fat for
winter, obese squirrels are
avid for our seeds.

Wednesday, November 11—Veterans Day

Who's thinking of vets?
Today starts the Christmas sales
season, dear shoppers.

Thursday, November 12

First time in a month
I didn't cook dinner. Thank
you, Silver Palace.

Friday, November 13

Too much to drink: It
is the last day of the past
of my life, please God.

Saturday, November 14

Husband-artist plays
with strange toys: leaves, bullets, glass
depict his vision.

Sunday, November 15

In the market, how
could I have brought so many
cookies and no bread??

~Middle-Aged Blues Cycle~

Monday, November 16

"You don't look like your
book's photo," she says (ten years
and ten pounds later).

Tuesday, November 17

Eighty-three rum balls
rolled in sugar, packed in tins
ready for Christmas.

Wednesday, November 18

I am a faithful
stay-at-home, breakfast-making
wife: A dinosaur.

Thursday, November 19

The Mighty Mean Reds,
I'd Rather-Be-Deads; only
hope is menopause.

Friday, November 20

Puss peeks from behind
the long-fronded plant, Rousseau's
cat in a green jungle.

Saturday, November 21

I need eyeglasses,
hair dye; cracked a crown today –
Woman falls apart.

Sunday, November 22

A mild-as-April
day surprises us in our
wintery habits.

Monday, November 23

After all the wind
and rain one last leaf clings still
to the maple tree.

Tuesday, November 24

Outrage of alarm
at 6:40; it's almost
past bearing to rise.

Wednesday, November 25

Oh kind, kind dentist.
He labors and I am no
longer snaggle-toothed.

Thursday, November 26

I am thankful for
Joe, my parents, and my cat.
I am not alone.

Friday, November 27

Shopping temptations —
books, clothes, and music — All I
bought was toys for Puss.

Saturday, November 28

Zola said artists
live out loud. I think that my
life is a whisper.

Sunday, November 29

Bread! onion rye, corn
muffins, crusty French, oatmeal,
pita, and sourdough!

Monday, November 30

I make woodstove fires
bake bread and pick blackberries
Ol' Backwoods Bessie.

十
二
月

Tuesday, December 1

Chubby striped raccoon
waddles through the yard, but finds
garbage cans emptied.

Wednesday, December 2

So cloudy gray, day
in day out; we are every
one becoming S.A.D.

Thursday, December 3

Silver tinsel rope,
golden stars to string in the
office for good cheer.

Friday, December 4

Guardian Angel:
the part of man that is (still?)
(already?) with God.

Saturday, December 5

Even a small snow
makes our land look right, dressed for
us in winter white.

Sunday, December 6

I've come to see that
I am boringly earnest,
a walking lecture.

Monday, December 7

The Importance of
Being Earnest? None at all;
I'd rather be Wilde.

Tuesday, December 8

Remembrance of Things
Past: Mother Proust says, "Marcel,
that's not how it was!"

Wednesday, December 9

"With my body I
thee worship." I release you
from that wedding vow.

Thursday, December 10

Room full of women
with bellies full of babies;
I am the thin one.

Friday, December 11

Visions of tubes and
uteri – not sugarplums –
dance in my aching head.

Saturday, December 12

Cartons of Christmas
cheer, gifts for our families,
hold back the terror.

Sunday, December 13

Thinking of Monday
and how much I am going
to enjoy peeing.

Monday, December 14

Humiliating
that my bladder won't behave
like other people's.

Tuesday, December 15

Kitty bats at the
little Christmas tree balls, a
new seasonal sport.

Wednesday, December 16

Relentless pressing
on my mind – call, call – and I
do, and something's wrong.

Thursday, December 17

Strange shapes on the screen
my insides ultrasounded
to their very deeps.

Friday, December 18

I pushed down my fear
so well I didn't know it
was there. Now I know.

Saturday, December 19

No critter wants the
fish and catnip treats Miss Puss
rejected. Oh, well.

Sunday, December 20—Hanukkah

little hope of snow
for Christmas, the present I
would like most to get

Monday, December 21—Winter Solstice

Even as winter
begins it begins to end
as days grow longer

Tuesday, December 22

time passes without
snow and we grow resigned to
a brown Christmas – Bah!

Wednesday, December 23

I don't like being
47, but think of
the alternative...

Thursday, December 24

Overnight, small snow
crept into town to whisper
its Merry Christmas

Friday, December 25—Christmas Day

Christmas cookies from
Gretchen, so comfortingly
the same every year

Saturday, December 26

Chestnuts smell of street
corners New York winters when
fifty cents counted

Sunday, December 27

Exploding jewels,
tube of Oohs and Wows, Christmas
gift Kaleidoscope

Monday, December 28

Hand-blown glass beads more
beautiful than gems, colors
from rainbow heaven

Tuesday, December 29

Bubbles and candy,
earrings and jeans, music and
a Very Big Book

Wednesday, December 30

I've been here before
but go on out of habit
hoping for newness

Thursday, December 31

Tiny Chickadees
try landing on the icy
deck and go s l i d i n g

Friday, January 1—New Year's Day

My Resolution
is to live this year with all
the courage I have

Saturday, January 2

She who runs out of
library books must pay five
dollars for a fix

Sunday, January 3

This is the year of
no winter, as the wooly
bear foretold last fall

Monday, January 4

Don't forget: You are
a unique person, just like
everybody else.
~Ann Landers classic~

Tuesday, January 5

Fragrance of orange,
rum and chocolate: making
happy birthday cake

Wednesday, January 6

A birthday always
holds magic; maybe we'll win
tonight's lottery!

Thursday, January 7

No, squirrel, don't come
in the house when I open
the door to feed you

Friday, January 8

There is life after
dinner when dinner doesn't
include any wine!

Saturday, January 9

My neighbor's gone to
Florida so I don't hear
the latest gossip

Sunday, January 10

The book stops here, but
I can't. I picked up my pen
and won't lay it down.

~The End~

Rita Randazzo published her first haiku poem at 17 in *American Haiku* magazine and has been writing haiku and other poetry ever since. She is the author of three poetry collections and two cookbooks and is currently at work on a new project in short-form writing. She lives in Vermont with her husband Joe.